# Inventing the Future

# Inventing the Future

## A PHOTOBIOGRAPHY OF

## Thomas Alva
# EDISON

BY MARFÉ FERGUSON DELANO

NATIONAL
GEOGRAPHIC
WASHINGTON, D. C.

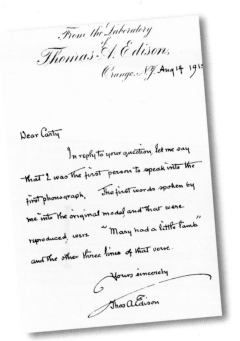

*From the Laboratory of Thomas A. Edison, Orange. N.J. Aug 14 1915*

Dear Canby

In reply to your question, let me say that I was the first person to speak into the first phonograph. The first words spoken by me into the original model and that were reproduced, were " Mary had a little lamb" and the other three lines of that verse.

Yours sincerely

Thos A Edison

A WORD ABOUT THE TYPE:
The font used for quotations, Hopper Josephine, has been specially chosen to approximate Edison's own handwriting, shown above in a letter.

The National Geographic Society is one of the world's largest nonprofit scientific and educational organizations. Founded in 1888 to "increase and diffuse geographic knowledge," the Society's mission is to inspire people to care about the planet. It reaches more than 400 million people worldwide each month through its official journal, *National Geographic*, and other magazines; National Geographic Channel; television documentaries; music; radio; films; books; DVDs; maps; exhibitions; live events; school publishing programs; interactive media; and merchandise. National Geographic has funded more than 10,000 scientific research, conservation, and exploration projects and supports an education program promoting geographic literacy.

For more information, please visit nationalgeographic.com, call 1-800-NGS LINE (647-5463), or write to the following address:

NATIONAL GEOGRAPHIC SOCIETY
1145 17th Street N.W.
Washington, D.C. 20036-4688 U.S.A.

Visit us online at nationalgeographic.com/books

For librarians and teachers: ngchildrensbooks.org

More for kids from National Geographic:
kids.nationalgeographic.com

For information about special discounts for bulk purchases, please contact National Geographic Books Special Sales:
ngspecsales@ngs.org

*For my parents, Marie and Forest Ferguson—MFD*

**Staff for this Book**
Bea Jackson, *Art Director*
Jennifer Emmett, *Project Editor*
Barbara Sheppard, *Illustrations Editor*
Marty Ittner, *Designer*
Callie Broaddus, *Associate Designer*
Suzanne Patrick Fonda, *Editor*
Jo H. Tunstall, *Assistant Editor*
Paige Towler, *Editorial Assistant*
Meredith Wilcox, *Illustrations Coordinator*
Carl Mehler, *Director of Maps*
Matt Chwastyk, Nicholas Rosenbach, *Map Research and Production*
Lewis R. Bassford, *Production Manager*
Bobby Barr, *Manager, Production Services*

**Published by the National Geographic Society**
Gary E. Knell, *President and CEO*
John M. Fahey, *Chairman of the Board*
Melina Gerosa Bellows, *Chief Education Officer*
Declan Moore, *Chief Media Officer*
Hector Sierra, *Senior Vice President and General Manager, Book Division*

**Senior Management Team, Kids Publishing and Media**
Nancy Laties Feresten, *Senior Vice President;* Jennifer Emmett, *Vice President, Editorial Director, Kids Books;* Julie Vosburgh Agnone, *Vice President, Editorial Operations;* Rachel Buchholz, *Editor and Vice President, NG Kids magazine;* Michelle Sullivan, *Vice President, Kids Digital;* Eva Absher-Schantz, *Design Director;* Jay Sumner, *Photo Director;* Hannah August, *Marketing Director;* R. Gary Colbert, *Production Director*

**Digital**
Anne McCormack, *Director;* Laura Goertzel, Sara Zeglin, *Producers;* Jed Winer, *Special Projects Assistant;* Emma Rigney, *Creative Producer;* Brian Ford, *Video Producer;* Bianca Bowman, *Assistant Producer;* Natalie Jones, *Senior Product Manager*

The Library of Congress cataloged the 2002 edition as follows:
Delano, Marfé Ferguson.
  Inventing the future : a photobiography of Thomas Alva Edison / by Marfé Ferguson Delano.
    p. cm.
Includes bibliographical references and index.
Summary: Presents a biography of the tireless Thomas Edison, illustrated with many photos of his life and inventions.
  ISBN 978-0-7922-6721-8
  1. Edison, Thomas A. (Thomas Alva), 1847-1931—Juvenile literature. 2. Inventors—United States—Biography—Juvenile literature. 3. Edison, Thomas A. (Thomas Alva), 1847-1931—Portraits—Juvenile literature. [1. Edison, Thomas A. (Thomas Alva), 1847-1931. 2. Inventors.] I. Title.
  T40.E25 D45 2002                                                    621.3'092—
dc21

                                        2001007357

2015 paperback edition ISBN: 978-1-4263-2220-4
2015 Reinforced Library Binding ISBN: 978-1-4263-2233-4

COVER: The famous inventor of the light bulb—Thomas Alva Edison
(COVER PHOTO CREDITS: Edison (front & back): Thomas Edison National Historical Park, light bulb: CreativeNature.nl/Shutterstock)
HALF-TITLE PAGE: A light bulb sketch from 1879
TITLE PAGE: Edison working at his drafting board
QUOTE PAGE: The inventor mixes chemicals in his West Orange laboratory.
BACK COVER: Edison slumps exhausted next to one of his great inventions—the phonograph.

National Geographic supports K–12 educators with ELA Common Core Resources. Visit natgeoed.org/commoncore for more information.

Printed in China
14/RRDS/1

"Genius is 1 percent inspiration and 99 percent perspiration."

Proud father Thomas Edison sits with daughter Madeleine and son Charles at Glenmont, their home in West Orange, New Jersey.

# FOREWORD

On a scrap of lined paper from my grandmother, Madeleine Edison—Thomas Edison's daughter—are the words: "What seems impossible today, may not be tomorrow.—Thomas A. Edison."

The impressions that came down to me of my great-grandfather are of an irrepressible inventor not merely of things but also of the systems that make things work, that better people's lives. He pressed himself to experiment, explore, devise, and creatively work toward improving dimensions of the physical world. His well-known comment that invention was 1 percent inspiration and 99 percent perspiration resonates with me when I think back on visiting his lab as a child and seeing the vast array, not only of chemicals but of other natural artifacts as well.

Edison's work produced more than a thousand patents, but not all of it really succeeded. He encountered many disappointments. He lost most of his fortune in the 1890s in mining ventures. He lost most of his factory in 1914 in a disastrous fire. Later he wrote on a singed picture of himself, the fire "never touched me!" and rebuilt the works. Edison was not daunted by failure. Failed experiments were not failures to him if they produced new information and eliminated blind alleys. Trying and failing became a system for thinking. His own experimental lab was the first of its kind and the harbinger of the modern research laboratory.

Every avenue of Edison's world offered opportunity, and he hoped others would seize on the challenges of engineering, chemistry, sound transmission, and other fields in that same spirit. Now more than ever, we Americans and, as Walt Whitman once put it, "Americans of all nations," must go forward with Thomas Edison's determination.

*David Edward Edison Sloane*

DAVID EDWARD EDISON SLOANE

Thomas Alva Edison never met a problem he didn't think he could solve. He was sure that if he worked hard enough and long enough at something, he would eventually discover a way to make it work. And he often did just that. In the process, he developed many inventions that would shape the way we live today.

Edison was born on February 11, 1847, in Milan, Ohio. His father, Samuel Edison, Jr., ran a shingle mill and grain business. His mother, Nancy Elliott Edison, was a schoolteacher before her marriage to Samuel. Thomas Alva was the last of their seven children, three of whom died in childhood. Called "Al" as a youngster, he was named for his great-uncle Thomas and for a family friend, Captain Alva Bradley.

When Edison was seven years old, his family moved to Port Huron, Michigan, a bustling port town on the southern tip of Lake Huron. Samuel ran a grocery store and worked in the grain and lumber businesses. He was always on the lookout for a way to make more money. Next to the family's house, he built a 100-foot-high wooden tower, which he promoted as a tourist attraction. Anyone willing to pay 25 cents could climb to its top and enjoy a bird's-eye view of the lake and surrounding countryside.

There was plenty to see in Port Huron. The town boasted lumber mills, shipyards, sawmills, and foundries, or iron factories. These industries used machinery that fascinated young Al, who by all accounts had a double dose of curiosity.

Like many children in 19th-century America, Al had little formal education. He attended an actual school for no more than a year

Thomas Edison was four years old when this portrait was made. Accounts of his boyhood recall that the young inventor-to-be amused himself by building little plank roads with scraps of lumber gathered from the sawmill.

"My mother taught me how to read good books quickly and correctly, and as this opened up a great world in literature, I have always been very thankful for this early training."

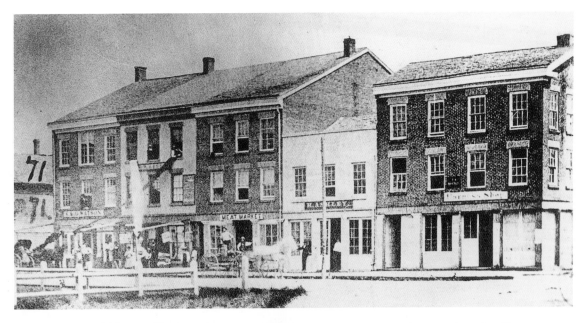

Edison was born in Milan, Ohio, in 1847, the same year this photograph of the town was taken.

When Edison was seven, his family moved to this house in Port Huron, Michigan. His father stands in the doorway.

or two. According to a story the inventor told later in life, one of his schoolmasters was angered by Al's tendency to daydream in class and one day called him "addled." When Al came home in tears about this, his mother acted swiftly. Edison later recalled, "I found out what a good thing a mother was, she brought me back to the school and angrily told the teacher that he didn't know what he was talking about. She was the most enthusiastic champion a boy ever had, and I determined right then that I would be worthy of her, and show her that her confidence had not been misplaced."

"My mother's ideas and mine differed at times, especially when I got experimenting and mussed up things."

Thomas Edison was the seventh and last child born to Nancy Elliott Edison and Samuel Edison, Jr.

Nancy took her son out of the school and took charge of his education herself. Under her guidance, Edison developed a deep love of reading, which stayed with him for the rest of his life. One of the most important books Edison read in his youth was a science textbook called *A School Compendium of Natural and Experimental Philosophy*. Among the topics the book covered were mechanics, acoustics, optics, electricity, magnetism, and astronomy. It also featured a description of the electric telegraph, at the time the fastest form of communication ever invented.

Merely reading the book, however, was not enough for Al. He had to try the experiments for himself, so he could learn exactly how things worked. He even built his own telegraph set based on an illustration in the book. Like other electrical instruments of the time, it drew electricity from batteries attached to it. Al stretched a wire from his house to a friend's, half a mile away, so that they could practice sending each other the dots and dashes of the Morse code over the telegraph.

When a book on chemistry seized his imagination, Al set up a labora-tory in the cellar of his house and gathered a large amount of chemicals to stock it. He spent many an hour mixing acids and other chemicals and alarming his parents with the occasional explosion.

Al was 12 years old when he talked his parents into letting him take a job aboard the Grand Trunk Railway, which had just opened a line in Port Huron. For the next four years, he sold newspapers including the *Detroit Free Press*, magazines, candy, peanuts, cigars, and other items to passengers on the daily round trip to Detroit. He also set up a stand at the Port Huron station to sell fruit and vegetables.

During the long layovers in Detroit, Al often passed the time in the library, reading all the books he could find on science and technology. His new job on the train didn't keep him from experimenting. He just performed his investigations in the baggage car. But when a chemical spilled and caught fire one day, the conductor put an end to his career as an onboard chemist.

When he was 14, Al set up a printing press in the baggage car and began publishing his own newspaper. It contained news of the day—which he picked up from telegraph operators at stations along the way—as well as train schedules, birth announcements, gossip, jokes, and market prices for butter, eggs, turkeys, and hogs. A subscription could be had for eight cents a month. One issue contained a headline that reflected his lifelong attitude toward work: "The more to do, the more done."

During the years he worked on the train, Edison noticed that his hearing was failing. Although never totally deaf, he gradually became very hard of hearing. Hearing loss seems to have run in his family. The condition might also have been caused by illness or injury. Whatever the cause, Edison did not look at his hearing loss as a disadvantage. On the contrary, he considered it an asset, saying that it helped him concentrate on his work and sleep without being disturbed by outside sounds.

Radiating confidence, Edison poses for the camera at about age 14. By this time he had noticed that his hearing was failing. He later remarked, "I have not heard a bird sing since I was 12 years old."

"The first station...was a small one where I generally sold two papers. I saw a crowd ahead on the platform, thought it some excursion, but the moment I landed there was a rush for me; then I realized that the telegraph was a great invention."

While working as a newsboy on the Grand Trunk Railway, Edison peddled papers at stations along the train's route, including this depot in Mt. Clemens, Michigan. He later rescued a toddler from an oncoming train at this station.

GRAND TRUNK RAILROAD

CHANGE OF TIME

## THE WEEKLY HERALD.

### PUBLISHED BY A. EDISON.

#### TERMS.

THE WEEKLY Eight Cents Per Month,

#### LOCAL INTELEGENCE.

Premium—We believe that the Grand Trunk Railway, give premiums, every 6 months to their Engineers, who use the least Wood and Oil, running the usual journey. Now we have rode with Mr. E. L. Northrop, one of their Engineers and we do not believe you could fall in with another Engineer, more careful, or attentive to his Engine, being the most steady driver that we have ever rode behind [and we consider ourselves some judge, having been Railway riding for over two years constantly.] always kind, and obliging, and ever at his post. His Engine we understand does not cost one fourth for repairs what the other Engines do. We would respectfully recommend him to the kindest consideration of the G. T. R. Officers.

The more to do the more done—We have observed along the line of railway at the different stations where there is only one Porter, such as at Utica, where he is fully engaged, from morning until late at night, that he has everything clean, and in first class order, even the platforms the snow does not lie for a week after it has fallen, but is swept off before it is almost down, at other stations where there is two Porters things are vica versa.

J. S. P. Hathaway runs a daily Stage from the station, to New Baltimore in connexion with all ....

Professor F.... r, has returned to Canada after entertaining delighted audiences at New Baltimore for the past two weeks listening to his comical lectures &c.

Didn't succeed—A gentleman by the name of Watkins agent for the Haytian goverment, recently tried to swindle the Grand Trunk Railway company out of sixty seven dollars the price of a valise he claimed to have lost at Sarnia, and he was well nigh successfull in the undertaking. But by the indominatable perseverance and energy of Mr. W. Smith, detective of the company. The case was cleared up in a very different style. It seems that the would be gentleman while crossing the river on the ferry boat, took the check off of his valise, and carried the valise in his hand, not forgeting to put the check in his pocket, the baggageman missed the baggage after leaving Port Huron. while looking over his book to see if he had every thing with him, but to his great surprise he lost one piece, he telegraphed back stating so, but no baggage could be found. It was therefore given into the hands of Mr Smith, to look after, in the meantime Mr Watkins wrote a letter to Mr Tubman, Agent at Detroit asking to be satisfied for the loss he had sustained in consequence, and refering Mr Tubman to Mr W.A.A. Howard Esq, of Detroit, and the Hon. Messrs Brown & Wilson of Toronto, for reference. We hardly know how such men are taken in with such traveling villians, but such is the case, meantime Mr Smith, cleared up the whole mystery by finding the lost valise in his posession, and the Haytian Agent offered to pay ten dollars for the troubles he had put the company to, and have the matter hushed over,

Not so, we feel that the villian should have his name posted up in the various R. R. in the ....

PT. HURON STATION,

An Omnibus leaves the Station for Pt. Huron, on the arrival of all Train

At age 15, Edison dropped his childhood nickname of Al, preferring to be
called Tom or Thomas. As he rode the
rails, he saw firsthand the value of the
telegraph—and one day he figured out
how to use it to his advantage. People
were always eager for news of the Civil
War, which had broken out the previous
year. When Edison arrived in Detroit on
April 6, 1862, he went as usual to the
offices of the *Detroit Free Press* to pick up

Published many years after the actual event,
a magazine illustration depicts the teenage
Edison saving a child from being crushed
by a train.

the newspapers he would sell on the ride back home. Hot off the press
was news of a bloody battle at Shiloh, Tennessee, where thousands of
soldiers had been killed or wounded.

Edison felt sure that if people knew about the battle, they would
want to buy a newspaper to read the details. So he hatched a plan.
First he persuaded the telegraph operator in Detroit to send news of
the battle to the telegraph offices in the stations along the train's route.
Then he bought 1,000 newspapers to sell, instead of the 100 he usually
purchased. When the train pulled into the stations, people anxious to
learn more about the battle crowded around to buy a paper. Not only
did Edison sell all of the 1,000 copies, he also raised the price of the
papers at each stop. By the time he got home to Port Huron, the few
papers he had left sold for five times their usual price. Edison later
recalled that not only did he make "what to me was an immense sum
of money" that day, he also "started the next day to learn telegraphy."

Edison turned over some of his newsboy duties to his friends and
began hanging around telegraph offices, watching the operators send
and receive messages. He yearned to become a telegraph operator himself.
One day, a twist of fate helped his dream come true. During a stop at
a small station, Edison rescued a three-year-old boy playing on the tracks

from an oncoming train. The child's father, a telegraph operator, offered to give Tom lessons in railroad telegraphy as a reward. Edison leaped at the opportunity, studied 18 hours a day, and soon landed a job as a telegraph operator in Port Huron.

Telegraph wires reached from coast to coast by this time. Invented by Samuel Morse in 1837, the telegraph was a sort of electric switch. Current passing through it could be turned on and off with the tap of a finger. Messages were created by sending long or short pulses of current through a telegraph at one end of a wire to another telegraph at the other end of the wire. At the receiving end of the wire, marks were indented on a roll of paper tape moving around a cylinder, a device called a Morse register. Long pulses made dashes, short pulses made dots. Morse created a code in which the dots and dashes represented the letters of the alphabet. Telegraph operators receiving a message translated the code into letters and wrote them down.

By the time Edison became a telegrapher in 1863, most telegraphs used a device called

### Tracing Edison's Path

CANADA U.S.

ONTARIO

MICHIGAN

Edison's boyhood home

Edison took his first job as a tramp telegrapher

Stratford

CANADA U.S.

Edison worked as a telegrapher and an inventor

Edison traveled here daily as a newsboy on the Grand Trunk Railway

Edison ran an iron mining operation, 1890-1900

Ogdensburg

NEW YORK

Boston• MASS.

Detroit• Port Huron

Newark

Edison's birthplace

•Milan

West Orange

Edison opened his first laboratory, 1870

IND.

OHIO

Edison bought the Glenmont estate in 1886, and opened a new laboratory in 1887

NEW JERSEY

Indianapolis•

Cincinnati•

New York

Edison worked as a tramp telegrapher

•Louisville

Edison worked as an inventor

KENTUCKY

TENNESSEE

Menlo Park

•Memphis

Edison opened his "invention factory," 1876

Edison worked as a tramp telegrapher

ATLANTIC OCEAN

LOUISIANA

•New Orleans

FLORIDA

Gulf of Mexico

Edison's winter home and laboratory

0  miles  200
0  km.  300

Fort Myers•

This map shows places associated with Edison. As a "tramp telegrapher," he worked in Stratford, Ontario, then followed jobs to Indianapolis, Cincinnati, Memphis, Louisville, and New Orleans. After working in Boston and New York, he opened his first laboratory in Newark, New Jersey.

a sounder instead of a register. The sounder created Morse code by transforming the pulses into audible clicks, with short and long intervals between them. Operators had to mentally translate the clicks into letters and words and write down the message by hand—a feat that required fast thinking and faster handwriting.

Pictured here during his "tramp telegrapher" days, Edison preferred to work night jobs, which he said gave him "more leisure to experiment."

Initially, the telegraph was used to send safety signals from train station to train station to prevent railway accidents. Soon, however, other kinds of information—including news reports and personal messages—crowded the lines. During the Civil War, the telegraph became a vital tool for military communications.

As the telegraph industry expanded, skilled operators were in great demand. At 16, Edison left Port Huron and set off on his own as a so-called "tramp telegrapher," taking jobs wherever a telegrapher was needed in cities throughout the Midwest and South. His skill and speed as an operator grew, which helped him land new jobs. Keeping them, however, was another matter.

Edison still had an irrepressible urge to experiment. It was part of a telegrapher's job to keep the equipment running, but that was too easily done for him to find it interesting. He couldn't resist tinkering with the machines to see how he might improve them. The chemicals used in the batteries that powered the telegraphs were also too tempting to pass up, so he conducted tests with them. Along the way, he learned a lot about how batteries and electricity worked. He also sometimes made a mess of the telegraph office and neglected his paid duties. Not surprisingly, his bosses frequently suggested that he move on. That was fine with Edison. He was eager to see more of the world and didn't want to settle down in one place for too long.

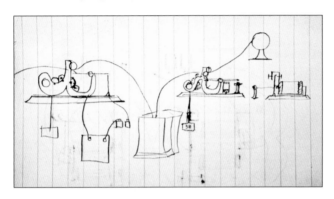

Edison drew this design for a telegraph practice instrument in 1867. Considered to be his first true invention, the device recorded a message at normal speed and then played it back at a slower pace.

Wherever he went, Edison continued to devour book after book. By now he was concentrating on volumes about electricity and telegraph technology. He preferred to work night jobs so that he could have the day to himself to read and experiment. This meant that he did not always get as much sleep as he needed. He started taking catnaps during the day, a practice he continued all his life.

In Indianapolis, Indiana, Edison set his sights on becoming a press operator, a highly paid and prestigious job. Press operators took down reports from news services and passed them along to newspaper publishers. Unfortunately, press copy came over the telegraph faster than he could write it down. Edison thought about this problem, then devised a solution. He figured that if he could receive the copy at a slower pace and get experience in writing it down, he could gradually increase the pace of the copy and thus his speed. So he devised a machine—considered his first true invention—to help him practice. Built with a pair of Morse registers, the instrument recorded a message at usual speed and then played it back at a slower speed.

"Anything that won't sell, I don't want to invent. Its sale is proof of utility, and utility is success."

Edison's electric vote recorder let lawmakers vote yes or no with the flip of a switch, then recorded and totaled the vote. But Edison could not sell the invention. Legislators preferred to cast their votes by voice.

In 1868, Edison took a job in the Western Union telegraph office in Boston. He found the city an exciting place. Not only did it have a large telegraphic community, it was filled with inventors. One of them was Alexander Graham Bell, who in 1876 would invent the telephone. Edison worked nights as a press operator and spent his days exploring the shops where telegraphs and other electrical devices were designed and made. Inspired by all the activity he found, Edison soon quit his job to focus full time on bringing out inventions. He met with people who had money to invest and persuaded them to provide the funds he needed to develop his ideas and have his inventions made. He specialized in telegraphic devices, but he also worked on other inventions.

When he was 22 years old, Edison received his first patent. It was for an electric vote recorder. A patent is an official document issued by the government that gives a person or company the sole right to make or sell an invention. Edison hoped the device would be used by state legislatures, but lawmakers were not interested in buying it. The experience taught him a valuable lesson: Never again would he invent something that people didn't want to buy.

"I had the faculty of sleeping in a chair any time for a few minutes at a time."

A taker of catnaps since his days as a young telegrapher, Edison wasn't picky about where he nodded off. Here he snoozes atop a lab table in his West Orange laboratory in 1911.

Manufactured at his Newark factory and embellished with his name, Edison's Universal Printer, a stock ticker, was among his first commercially successful inventions.

In 1869, Edison moved to New York City. Many telegraph companies, including Western Union, had their headquarters in the city, which brimmed with business opportunities for an ambitious young inventor. Edison worked for a while for the Laws Gold Indicator Company, where he repaired and improved the company's stock printers. Also called stock tickers because of the noise they made, stock printers were a kind of telegraph that sent minute-by-minute reports of the changing price of gold to stockbrokers' offices.

That fall, Edison started a business called Pope, Edison and Company with a fellow inventor named Franklin Pope. They advertised themselves as electrical engineers who could "devise electrical instruments and solve problems to order." The company offered a variety of services having to do with telegraph technology and was also committed to bringing out new devices—Edison's specialty. He patented a number of telegraphic improvements that were eagerly bought by the telegraph industry. Finally he was inventing what people wanted and were willing to pay for.

By the age of 23, Edison had earned a reputation as one of the best electrical inventors in the country, which helped him attract more financial backers. In 1870, his partnership with Pope broke up, and Edison opened his very own manufacturing company and laboratory in Newark, New Jersey.

Employees gather for a group photograph in front of Edison's Newark factory while a figure—
believed to be Edison himself—looks out from a top window.

Edison hired more than 50 employees to make and sell his stock printers and other equipment and to assist with his many experiments. Among
the skilled machinists and clockmakers he hired were Charles Batchelor
and John Kruesi. A British-born machinist and draftsman, Batchelor
soon became Edison's right-hand man as well as his friend. They worked
closely together for nearly 25 years. Kruesi, born in Switzerland and
trained as a clockmaker, worked with Edison for 20-some years.

In the fall of 1871, 24-year-old Edison started his own news service,
the News Reporting Telegraph Company. Among the company's employe-
ees was a pretty 16-year-old clerk named Mary Stilwell, a Newark girl
whose father worked in a sawmill. Edison set his sights on Mary, and
after a brief courtship, they married on Christmas Day, 1871. When the

couple's first child was born, a daughter named Marion, Edison nicknamed her "Dot," after the telegraph signal. Their second child, Thomas Alva, Jr., was dubbed "Dash," of course. The Edisons' third child was named—and called—William.

Soon after their marriage, Mary discovered that she played second fiddle to her husband's true love—inventing. He often spent several days straight at the lab, working through the nights and catching naps on a workbench or desktop when exhaustion overwhelmed him. Whenever Edison was involved with a project, he became totally wrapped up in it. And since he almost always had dozens of inventions going at once, he had little time for anything else.

In Newark, Edison first developed the method of team inventing that would characterize the rest of his career. Whenever a new idea for an invention inspired him, he sketched it out in a notebook and then shared the drawing with Batchelor and Kruesi or other trusted assistants. Their job was to take the sketch and see that it was made into a working model. Lab workers then experimented with the model to see how the invention worked—or did not

Mary Stilwell (top) married Edison on Christmas Day, 1871. The couple had three children: Marion (middle), Thomas Alva, Jr. (bottom right), and William (bottom left).

The electric pen was among the inventions Edison developed and manufactured at his Newark facility. An advertisement for the device claimed that it could produce "5,000 copies from a single writing."

work, which was often the case. Edison was not discouraged when things went wrong. He and his workers would just keep trying until they found out what did work.

Edison's workers tended to be very loyal to "the old man," as they called their young boss. They admired and respected him for the way he worked alongside them, plunging into the dirtiest jobs with enthusiasm and putting in longer hours than anyone else. Moreover, Edison could be generous. He often gave assistants who worked closely with him on an invention a percentage of the profits it made.

Although Edison's Newark laboratory focused mainly on devices that improved the speed and efficiency of the telegraph, other electrical inventions were also under development. One of these was the electric pen, which could create multiple copies of a handwritten document. Business owners, from lawyers to mapmakers, immediately saw the value of the device, and it sold well. Although Edison manufactured and sold many of his inventions, he also sold the patents for many others. This gave the buyer the exclusive right to make and sell a device. Despite the income this generated, Edison was usually short of cash. That's because he tended to spend most of what he earned from one invention on the next.

In 1876, Edison sold his Newark business. He moved his family and about 20 of his best workers—including Batchelor and Kruesi—to a small farming village in New Jersey called Menlo Park, located about 20 miles from New York City. There he had a two-story laboratory built to his design. Unlike most other labs of the time, which combined inventing with manufacturing, Edison's new laboratory was devoted exclusively to researching and developing his ideas. It contained well-equipped chemistry and electrical labs and a machine shop for making models of his inventions. Edison often referred to the place as his "invention factory." He bragged that it would turn out "a minor invention every ten days and a big thing every six months or so."

Edison and his "muckers," as he fondly called his crew of fellow experimenters, lived up to the boast. Known as the "Chief Mucker," Edison patented 75 different inventions in the first two years at Menlo Park. Among them was an improved version of Alexander Graham Bell's telephone.

The biggest problem with Bell's telephone was that the sound it transmitted, or sent, was weak. A caller had to shout into it in order to be heard on the other end of the line. Edison felt sure he could not only find a way to make the telephone sound louder and clearer, he also could make it send messages over longer distances. Eager to gain the advantage in the budding telephone industry, Western Union hired him to do just that.

Edison knew that improving the transmitter—the device that converts the sound of a speaker's voice into electrical signals—was the key to better quality sound. The challenge was to find the material that would work best in it.

In 1877, less than a year after Bell's invention of the telephone, Edison discovered that tiny pieces of carbon encased in a small container, or button, gave the best results. Called the carbon button transmitter, the invention not only produced excellent sound, but greatly increased the range of the telephone. A version of it is still used in most telephones today.

"This [the phonograph] is my baby and I expect it to grow up to be a big feller and support me in my old age."

In 1878, Edison demonstrated his phonograph at the National Academy of Sciences in Washington, D.C. While there, he posed with his invention for this photograph taken by famed Civil War photographer Matthew Brady.

Edison (seated at center wearing a cap and scarf) and his muckers take a break in his Menlo Park "invention factory." Among the projects he worked on there was an improved telephone transmitter. To find the material that would work best in it, Edison and crew experimented with more than 2,000 different substances, including rubber, ivory, tobacco leaf, and fish bladder. "Every wrong attempt discarded," Edison declared, "is another step forward."

"Suggestions generally came from me. If any change was to be made, my assistants would speak to me about it, and if I thought best the change was made."

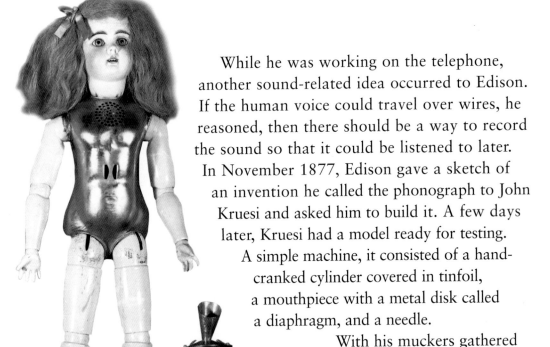

While he was working on the telephone, another sound-related idea occurred to Edison. If the human voice could travel over wires, he reasoned, then there should be a way to record the sound so that it could be listened to later. In November 1877, Edison gave a sketch of an invention he called the phonograph to John Kruesi and asked him to build it. A few days later, Kruesi had a model ready for testing.

A simple machine, it consisted of a hand-cranked cylinder covered in tinfoil, a mouthpiece with a metal disk called a diaphragm, and a needle.

With his muckers gathered around him, Edison turned the handle of the machine while he shouted a nursery rhyme into the mouthpiece. As the sound waves of his voice vibrated the diaphragm, the attached needle scratched grooves in the foil. When he finished reciting, he rewound the cylinder, put the needle into the tracks it had made, and cranked the handle again. To everyone's surprise, the machine worked the very first time! Out of the phonograph came Edison's voice, faint but clear: "Mary had a little lamb, its fleece was white as snow, and everywhere that Mary went, the lamb was sure to go." The excited experimenters stayed up all night recording themselves with the invention, which was the ancestor of modern CD players.

One of the uses Edison envisioned for the phonograph was a talking doll, which he began manufacturing in 1889. The doll's hollow tin body contained a miniature phonograph, shown here beside the doll. When the crank was turned, the doll "spoke" the words—usually a nursery rhyme—recorded on the tiny cylinder. Unfortunately, the mechanism proved too fragile to work reliably, so Edison shut down production of the toy.

**TRIUMPH**
Model A

**STANDARD**
Model A

**HOME**
Model A and B

**GEM**
Model A

**TRIUMPH**
Model B

**GEM**
Model B and C

**GEM**
Model D and E

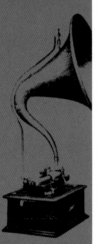
**TRIUMPH**
Model C and D

**GEM**

**TRIUMPH**
Model E, F and

**STANDARD**
Model E, F and G

**FIRESIDE**
Model B

Over the years, Edison produced a variety of phonographs for home use.
The records he made to play on them were delivered to homes (top) and could
also be bought in stores (bottom).

Paying customers listen through earphones to a recording in a "phonograph parlor" in Salina, Kansas, in the 1890s. Edison manufactured phonographs with a special coin-in-slot device for use in saloons and other places of entertainment.

The next morning Edison took his brand-new "baby" to New York City and dazzled the editors of *Scientific American* magazine with a demonstration. Word of the amazing invention spread rapidly, and Edison became a celebrity overnight. The phonograph's ability to reproduce human speech seemed like a miracle. Newspaper headlines proclaimed him the "Inventor of the Age" and the "Wizard of Menlo Park."

Edison, who enjoyed the attention the phonograph attracted, envisioned a variety of commercial uses for the device, including toys and dictation machines. He soon set it aside, however, to concentrate on the greatest challenge of his career—the development of an electric lighting system that could be used in homes and businesses.

Electric lighting was not a new idea. Brightly burning lamps called arc lights (which glowed when a current of electricity jumped between two carbon rods) had already replaced gas street lamps in some large cities by the 1870s. But they were not suitable for home use. Not only was their glare too intense for indoors, they were also smelly. So people still used candles, oil lamps, or gas lamps to light their homes after dark.

Aware that other inventors were racing toward the same goal as he, Edison vowed to get there first. To gain the financial support he needed, he took a gamble. In September 1878, he announced to reporters that he was very close to developing a practical incandescent lamp, or light bulb. Not only that, he said he expected to have a safe, affordable electric lighting system ready to go in just six weeks. He was exaggerating his progress greatly, but so strong was his reputation at the time that few questioned his claim. Confident of Edison's genius, several

The front page of *The Daily Graphic* from July 9, 1879, (top) pictures Edison in sorcerer's garb, a reference to his nickname, the "Wizard of Menlo Park." The cartoon at bottom illustrates the fear electrical wiring inspired in some people in the 1880s.

35

A replica of Edison's first successful light bulb, which glowed for more than 13 hours

rich investors established the Edison Electric Light Company to cover his expenses. Edison's gamble paid off. It was time for the real work to begin.

The groundwork for the incandescent light bulb had been laid many years earlier by an English chemist named Sir Humphry Davy. In 1802, Davy discovered that by passing an electric current through strips of metal, he could make them hot enough to glow brightly, or incandesce, for a few seconds before they burned up.

The Menlo Park lab hummed with round-the-clock activity as Edison and his muckers—including several newly hired electrical experts—tackled the problem of the light bulb. Edison set some of his associates the task of finding a way to get all the air out of the glass bulb, so that the material giving off the light, called the filament, would not burn up too quickly. Other workers tested more than 1,600 materials—including horsehair, coconut fibers, fish line, spider webs, and even the hair from John Kruesi's beard—to find the best filament.

Finally his persistence was rewarded. In the fall of 1879, Edison and his muckers tested a piece of cotton sewing thread. First they carbonized it by baking it until it charred and turned into carbon. Then they inserted the carbonized thread into the glass bulb, forced out the air with a special vacuum pump, and sealed the glass. When connected to an electric current, the bulb glowed steadily for more than 13 hours! Within a few weeks, the lab had produced an improved bulb that burned many hours longer.

In late December 1879, Edison invited the public to Menlo Park to see his marvelous new invention. As visitors got off the train in the evening, they were astounded by the brightly shining electric street lamps lighting their way. Even more impressive was the laboratory, which one newspaper article described as "brilliantly illuminated with twenty-five lamps."

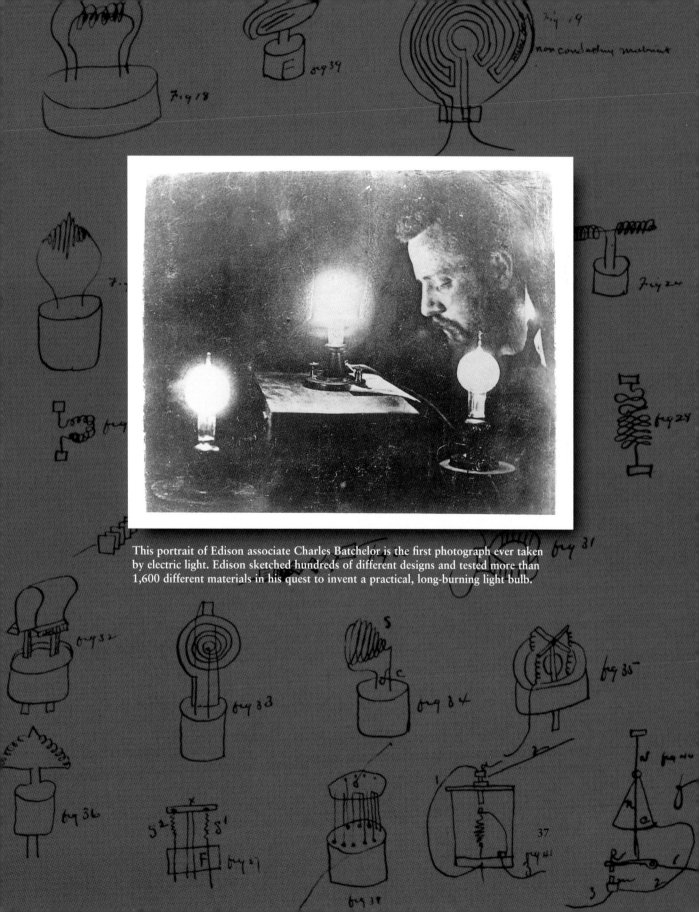

This portrait of Edison associate Charles Batchelor is the first photograph ever taken by electric light. Edison sketched hundreds of different designs and tested more than 1,600 different materials in his quest to invent a practical, long-burning light bulb.

37

A worker takes a break from laying underground cables for the Pearl Street power station in New York City. Edison himself often rolled up his sleeves and helped dig the trenches for the cables.

Over the next two years, Edison and his crew worked feverishly to invent the many other devices besides the light bulb that were needed to get a full lighting system up and running. At the top of the list was an efficient generator, or dynamo, to produce the electricity. They also developed wires and cables to deliver the electricity from the generators, which would be housed in central power stations, to streets and buildings. Sockets, switches, safety fuses, and lamp fixtures also had to be designed. Ever practical, Edison didn't forget to devise a meter to measure the amount of electricity that customers used, so they could be charged accordingly. His lighting would be cheap, yes, but not free!

By 1882, Edison had set up the world's first commercially successful electric power station, on Pearl Street in New York City. He and his family had moved to the city sometime earlier, so that he could personally supervise the installation of his lighting system. On September 4 of that year, he was finally ready to deliver what he had promised four years earlier. Standing in the office of millionaire businessman J. P. Morgan—one of his investors—Edison flicked a switch and current from the Pearl Street station lit the office lamps.

By nightfall, some two dozen buildings in the city's financial district glowed with Edison's electric lights. As crowds gathered in the streets to marvel at the latest magic from the Wizard of Menlo Park, his fame soared even higher.

Edison devoted the next few years to improving his electrical system and spreading it around the country and the world. He set up numerous companies to handle the manufacturing and installation of his products and made millions of dollars. Sadness intruded upon his success in 1884, however, when Mary died unexpectedly at the age of 29.

In 1885, Edison was introduced by friends to a young woman named Mina Miller, with whom he soon fell in love. In contrast to Mary, who came from a working-class background, Mina was the well-educated daughter of very wealthy parents, Lewis and Mary Miller, of Akron, Ohio. Lewis Miller, an inventor himself, had made his fortune improving and manufacturing harvesting machines.

With his second wife, Mina Miller (top), Edison had three children: Madeleine, Charles, and Theodore. On the Fourth of July, 1900, he entertained them with special firecrackers he made himself (bottom).

Edison's main laboratory in West Orange, New Jersey, contained machine shops, stock rooms, offices, an engine room, an electrical-testing room, a glass-blowing room, and a three-tiered library with 10,000 books. Edison liked to joke that he had stocked his new lab with "everything from an elephant's hide to the eyeballs of a United States Senator."

Edison taught 19-year-old Mina the Morse code so that they might "talk" to each other secretly when others were around. According to family legend, one day he tapped a question into her hand: "Will you marry me?" To his delight, she signaled back "Yes."

After their wedding in February 1886, Edison and Mina moved to West Orange, New Jersey, where he had purchased a 29-room mansion called Glenmont for his bride. Like many men of his day, Edison was not closely involved with his children. He turned over the upbringing of the three youngsters to their stepmother. In time, Mina had three children of her own with Edison: Madeleine, Charles, and Theodore.

The following year, Edison built the laboratory of his dreams. Located about a mile from Glenmont, it was the largest, best-equipped research facility in the world. Ten times bigger than Menlo Park, the main lab was three stories high and 250 feet long. Housed in separate buildings were a physics lab, a chemistry lab, and a metallurgical lab. In his new laboratory, Edison continued to improve his lighting system.

Edison's West Orange lab also contributed to the birth of the motion picture industry. Around 1889, Edison and a team of muckers led by William K. L. Dickson started work on "an instrument which does for the Eye what the phonograph does for the Ear."

Edison's earliest movies, such as this footage of a man sneezing, were filmed in West Orange. They were viewed through a peephole machine called a kinetoscope (inset).

Covered with tar paper, the "Black Maria" at Edison's lab in West Orange was the world's first motion picture studio. Named for its resemblance to a police paddy wagon, the structure could be turned on a circular track to follow the course of the sun. The roof opened up to let sunlight shine on the stage during filming.

"I am experimenting upon an instrument which does for the Eye what the phonograph does for the Ear, which is the recording and reproduction of things in motion."

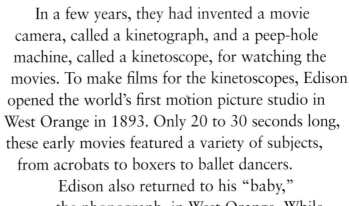

In a few years, they had invented a movie camera, called a kinetograph, and a peep-hole machine, called a kinetoscope, for watching the movies. To make films for the kinetoscopes, Edison opened the world's first motion picture studio in West Orange in 1893. Only 20 to 30 seconds long, these early movies featured a variety of subjects, from acrobats to boxers to ballet dancers.

Edison also returned to his "baby," the phonograph, in West Orange. While Edison had been working on electric lights, inventors Chichester Bell (a cousin of Alexander Graham Bell) and Charles Tainter had created their own, improved version of the machine, which used wax cylinders rather than tinfoil for recording. Spurred by the competition, Edison developed an even better wax-cylinder phonograph. Although he originally envisioned the device as a business machine for taking dictation, people were eager to purchase it for home entertainment. Edison was happy to satisfy them.

Not only did he produce a variety of phonographs for home use over the next 40 years, he also made pre-recorded cylinders, or records, of popular tunes to play on them. In the process, he helped to create what we now call the recording industry.

At the same time he was working on the phonograph and motion pictures, Edison embarked on a totally different venture. In 1890 he bought an iron mine near Ogdensburg, New Jersey

Edison patented a design for a poured-concrete house, and he even built concrete furniture, such as this ornate phonograph cabinet. Neither idea caught on with the public.

New York City's Yankee Stadium is nicknamed the "House That Ruth Built," in honor of baseball great Babe Ruth, but it was actually built using Edison Portland cement. Cement from Edison's plant was also used in the construction of the Panama Canal.

(which was later renamed Edison), with the goal of developing a new method of separating iron ore from rock and sand. Ten years and millions of dollars later, Edison shut down his mining operation when newly discovered sources of high-grade iron ore in the Midwest drove down the price he could get for his ore. Despite significant financial losses, he remained upbeat about the experience. "Well, it's [the money's] all gone," he remarked to an associate, "but we had a hell of a good time spending it."

Edison was able to use some of the rock-crushing techniques he developed at the mine when he entered the cement business around the turn of the century. Cement produced at the Edison Portland Cement Company was used for countless roads and buildings, including Yankee Stadium, a famous baseball park in New York City.

About 1900, Edison gave his West Orange muckers yet another task: Build a better storage battery for use in electric automobiles. A decade later, after experimenting with hundreds of different substances and

Ready for a road test, an automobile powered by Edison's storage battery bears a sign proclaiming its 1,000-mile goal. Edison stands beside the car. Seated in it are the test driver and an Edison company engineer.

techniques, they finally produced a workable alkaline battery. By then, most cars were gasoline powered and couldn't use Edison's battery. It did, however, have plenty of other uses. It worked well for lighting railway cars and signals and miners' lamps. It was also widely used in electric trucks. The military used it to light ships and power torpedoes. In fact, the nickel-iron alkaline storage battery ended up becoming the biggest moneymaker of all Edison's products.

In 1914, a fire swept through much of the West Orange complex. Although the main lab was spared, many of the surrounding factory buildings were badly damaged or destroyed. Instead of being depressed by the disaster, Edison saw it as an opportunity. He immediately started supervising the rebuilding of the complex. Not only did he make certain that the new buildings were better than ever, he had them constructed out of reinforced concrete to make them more fireproof.

When World War I broke out, Edison was asked by the secretary of the Navy to head the Naval Consulting Board. This group of the country's leading inventors and scientists was organized to investigate new

On a 1918 camping trip to West Virginia, Edison poses at an old gristmill with friends, including John Burroughs and Henry Ford (atop the wheel) and Harvey Firestone (far right).

In response to a letter asking him for the secrets to his success, Edison wrote, "I work 18 hours daily—have been doing this for 45 years." Even when his health began to fail in the 1920s, the inventor continued to punch in and out at his laboratory nearly every day.

*"I am sixty-seven, but I'm not too old to make a fresh start."*

Thomas and Mina Edison in 1908. Mina said later in life that "my job has been always to take care of Mr. Edison…. And we have tried to organize our home and our home life to give results just as much as the laboratory."

military technology. During the war, Edison spent much of his time working on techniques for detecting submarines.

A camping trip Edison took with automobile maker Henry Ford and tire manufacturer Harvey Firestone in 1916 was so enjoyable that it evolved into an annual adventure. Traveling by car—and accompanied by cooks, tent-pitchers, and other servants—the famous friends journeyed to a variety of destinations over the years, including New England, Michigan, Virginia, and the Great Smoky Mountains. Naturalist John Burroughs accompanied them on several trips and delighted in teaching his companions about nature. One summer President Warren G. Harding joined Edison and his cronies!

Although his health began to fail in the 1920s, Edison continued to work nearly every day. At his West Orange laboratory, he punched in and out with his own time card, just like the rest of the muckers. In the late 1920s, he took on a brand-new project. At the request of his friends Henry Ford and Harvey Firestone, Edison started a search for a new source of

natural rubber for use in car tires. With his usual thoroughness, he tested thousands of different plants. Even on his annual camping trips Edison continued the hunt, exploring the woods for plants with milky sap that just might be used to make rubber.

Edison conducted a great deal of his rubber research in the chemical laboratory at his winter estate in Fort Myers, Florida. There, in his large experimental garden, he grew more than a thousand varieties of plants.

Eventually Edison narrowed the candidates down to the wildflower commonly known as goldenrod, which had the advantage of growing and maturing quickly.

At his winter estate in Fort Myers, Florida, Edison and an associate examine a sample of goldenrod. The inventor hoped to make rubber from the plant's sap.

"I have accomplished all I promised."

"Negative results are just what I want. They're just as valuable to me as positive results. I can never find the thing that does the job best until I find the ones that don't do."

Still a night owl at age 65, Edison and his muckers—dubbed the Insomnia Squad—share a meal in the West Orange lab after working through the evening into the wee hours of the morning.

Edison attends to business in the library at his West Orange laboratory. The large paneled room served as the inventor's office, where he met with company executives and interviewed job-seekers. It was also something of a trophy room, a place to hang certificates and awards and photographs of notable moments in his life. His favorite part of the lab, however, was his private experimental room on the second floor.

Although he succeeded in making rubber from the plant, it was never manufactured for commercial use, in part because of the development of synthetic rubber.

To mark the 50th anniversary of Edison's electric light in 1929, Henry Ford organized a celebration in Dearborn, Michigan, where he had rebuilt Edison's Menlo Park laboratory as a museum. Among those who came to honor the 82-year-old inventor were President Herbert Hoover, airplane pioneer Orville Wright, and physicist Marie Curie. As part of the festivities, dubbed "Light's Golden Jubilee," Edison reenacted the lighting of the first incandescent lamp. In response to the lavish tributes offered him by numerous dignitaries, Edison praised his muckers. "When you honor me," he said, "you are also honoring the vast army of workers but for whom my work would have gone for nothing."

Edison continued inventing to the very end—he pursued his rubber experiments until a few months before his death. In the early morning hours of October 18, 1931, with his family gathered around him at Glenmont, he passed away from complications related to diabetes and other illnesses.

After his death, Edison's body lay in state in the library of his West Orange laboratory for two days and nights. During that time, more than fifty thousand people filed by to bid final farewell to the famous inventor.

Thomas Edison's funeral, a private ceremony, was held on October 21, 1931. That evening, in response to a request from President Herbert Hoover, people all across the United States paid their last respects to the "Inventor of the Age": At 10 p.m. Eastern time, they turned off their electric lights for one full minute.

In a rare moment of relaxation, Edison sits on the lawn of his West Orange estate, Glenmont. In 1922 the inventor was named "The Greatest Living American" in a *New York Times* poll.

# AFTERWORD

For Thomas Edison, inventing was nearly as natural and necessary as breathing. His imagination overflowed with all sorts of innovative ideas, and from the time he was a boy until shortly before his death, he never stopped experimenting. In his 84 years of life, Edison was granted an astounding 1,093 United States patents—a feat matched by no other inventor before or since. More than a third of the patents he received were related to what Edison considered his greatest achievement: the electric light and power system.

By bringing electricity into homes and businesses, Edison transformed the way people lived. Electric lights were just the beginning. Machines in factories were soon being powered by electricity, as were elevators and office tools, ranging from typewriters to dentists' drills. In the home, electric irons, vacuum cleaners, and other appliances helped lighten household chores.

Some historians contend that Edison's best invention of all was the state-of-the-art laboratory he set up in Menlo Park, where he and his muckers worked as a team to bring new ideas into reality. The first of its kind, Menlo Park became the model for the research and development labs that are now considered essential in many of today's industries.

Edison holds one of the
countless bulbs with which
he experimented. When he first
turned his attention to creating
a safe lighting system back in
1878, the inventor declared that
"the electric light is the light
of the future—and it will be my
light." History proved him true,
and electric light has ever since
been linked to his name.

57

With Mina on one side and President Herbert Hoover on the other, Edison (center, in dark hat) arrives in Dearborn, Michigan, for "Light's Golden Jubilee" in October 1929.

Thanks to such public-pleasing inventions as the phonograph, the light bulb, and the motion picture camera, Edison gained both fame and fortune. In his later years he was regarded as a national hero. Indeed, in 1928 he was awarded the congressional Medal of Honor for his many contributions to modern life. Although proud of his accomplishments,

This lab sketch from 1879 expresses the jubilation felt by Edison and his Menlo Park muckers at finally producing a long-burning light bulb.

As part of the 1929 Jubilee, Edison (seated) reenacts the lighting of his famous bulb 50 years earlier. Looking on are Henry Ford (standing, left) and former Edison employee Francis Jehl.

Edison had little patience with anyone who attributed his success to genius. "Sticking to it is the genius!" he insisted. Another time he remarked that "genius is 1 percent inspiration and 99 percent perspiration." Edison believed he could discover the solution to a new invention through sheer hard work and persistence. Luckily for us, he usually did.

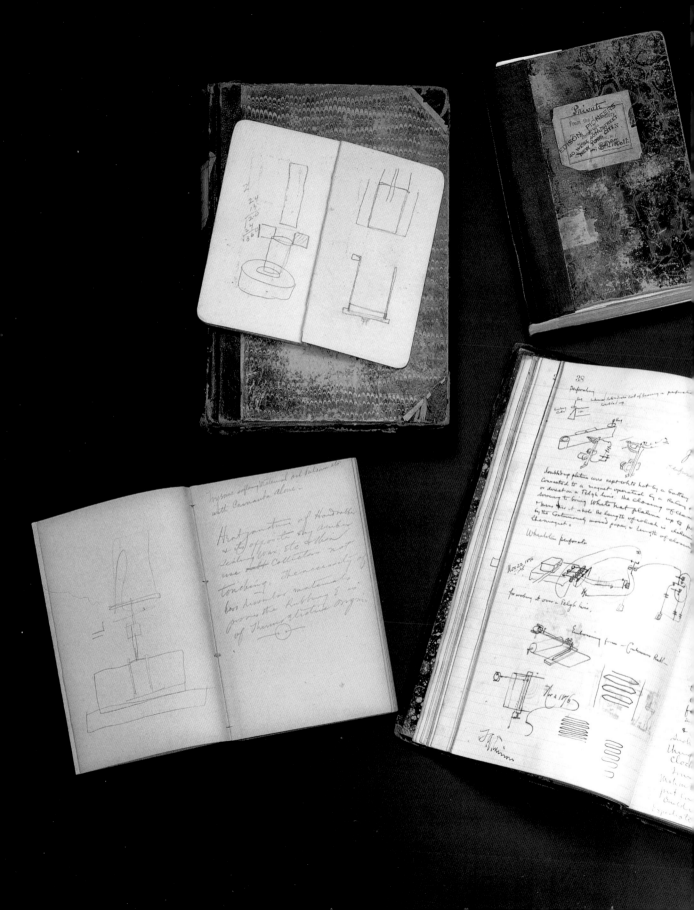

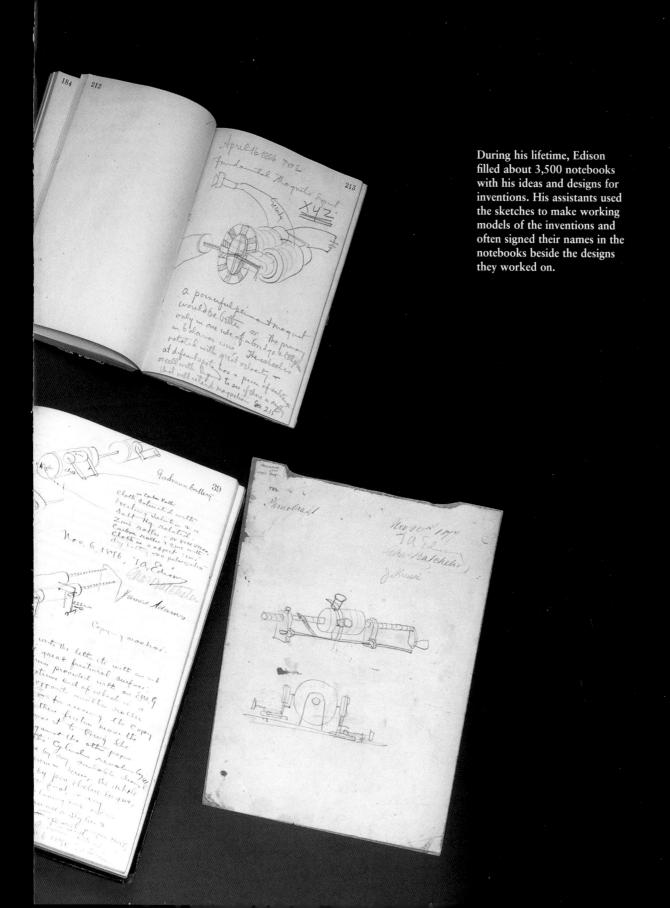

During his lifetime, Edison filled about 3,500 notebooks with his ideas and designs for inventions. His assistants used the sketches to make working models of the inventions and often signed their names in the notebooks beside the designs they worked on.

# CHRONOLOGY

### February 11, 1847
Thomas Alva Edison is born in Milan, Ohio

### 1854
Edison family moves to Port Huron, Michigan

### 1859
Takes job selling newspapers and candy on Grand Trunk Railway

### 1862
Learns how to operate telegraph equipment

### 1863-1867
Drifts from town to town working as a telegraph operator and inventing improvements for telegraphic equipment

Edison phonograph from 1911

### 1868
Moves to Boston; applies for his first patent, for the electric vote recorder

### 1869
Arrives in New York City; invents improved stock printer

### 1870
Opens a small laboratory and manufacturing facility in Newark, New Jersey

### December 25, 1871
Marries Mary Stilwell

### 1875
Develops quadruplex telegraph and sells patent for $30,000

### 1876
Moves his laboratory to Menlo Park, New Jersey

### 1877
Invents carbon-button telephone transmitter and the tinfoil phonograph

### October 1879
Creates first practical light bulb

### September 1882
Opens Pearl Street power station in New York City

### August 9, 1884
Wife Mary Stilwell Edison dies at age 29

### February 24, 1886
Marries Mina Miller and moves with his bride to West Orange, New Jersey

Thomas Edison marketed wax cylinders, precursors to today's CDs, with his own picture on the packaging.

### 1887
Opens new laboratory and factory facility in West Orange

### 1888
Improved phonograph ready for production; starts research on kinetograph and kinetoscope

### 1900-1910
Develops storage battery for use in electric cars and trucks

### 1915–1921
Heads the Naval Consulting Board

### 1927
Tries to find a new source of natural rubber

### 1928
Awarded Medal of Honor for his many contributions

### 1929
Fiftieth anniversary of light bulb celebrated at reconstructed Menlo Park lab in Dearborn, Michigan

### October 18, 1931
Thomas Alva Edison dies of complications from diabetes and other illnesses

### August 24, 1947
Mina Miller Edison dies

# RESOURCES

Quotes from Thomas Edison are taken from the following sources, which are cited below: *Edison: A Life of Invention*, by Paul Israel; *Edison: Inventing the Century*, by Neil Baldwin; *Thomas A. Edison: A Streak of Luck*, by Robert Conot; the Edison National Historic Site; and the Lemelson Center, Smithsonian Institution.

## BOOKS

BALDWIN, NEIL. *Edison: Inventing the Century*. New York: Hyperion, 1995.

CONOT, ROBERT. *Thomas A. Edison: A Streak of Luck*. New York: Da Capo Press, Inc.,1979.

ISRAEL, PAUL. *Edison: A Life of Invention*. New York: John Wiley & Sons, Inc., 1998.

## BOOKS WRITTEN ESPECIALLY FOR YOUNG READERS

MORGAN, NINA. *Thomas Edison*. New York: The Bookwright Press, 1991.

PARKER, STEVE. *Thomas Edison and Electricity*. New York: HarperCollins Publishers, 1992.

WALLACE, JOSEPH. *The Lightbulb*. New York: Atheneum Books for Young Readers, 1999.

## MAGAZINE ARTICLE

KRAUTWURST, TERRY. "When I Was a Kid: Childhood Experiences of Famous People." *National Geographic World* (April 1999) p. 28.

## VIDEOS

"Edison's Miracle of Light." The American Experience. Public Broadcasting Service, 1995.

"The Edison Effect." The History Channel. A&E Television Networks, 1995.

## WEB SITES

**Edison Birthplace Museum**
http://www.tomedison.org/

**Edison-Ford Winter Estates**
http://www.edison-ford-estate.com/index2.php3

**Edison National Historic Site**
http://www.nps.gov/edis/home.htm

**Edison's Miracle of Light, the American Experience, Public Broadcasting Service**
http://www.pbs.org/wgbh/amex/edison/index.html

**Henry Ford Museum & Greenfield Village**
http://www.hfmgv.org/histories/edison/tae.html

**Innovative Lives, Lemelson Center, Smithsonian Institution**
http://www.si.edu/lemelson/centerpieces/ilives/edisonil.html

**Inventing Entertainment, American Memory, Library of Congress**
http://memory.loc.gov/ammem/edhtml/edhome.html

**Thomas A. Edison Papers, Rutgers University**
http://edison.rutgers.edu/

## PLACES TO VISIT

**Edison Birthplace Museum**
9 Edison Drive
Milan, Ohio 44846
(419) 499-2135
*The house where Edison was born.*

**Edison-Ford Winter Estates**
2350 McGregor Boulevard
Fort Myers, Florida 33901
(914) 334-7419
*Edison's winter home, botanical gardens, and laboratory as well as the winter home of his friend Henry Ford.*

**Edison National Historic Site**
Main Street & Lakeside Avenue
West Orange, New Jersey 07052
(973) 736-0550
*Edison's West Orange laboratory and his home, Glenmont.*

**Henry Ford Museum & Greenfield Village**
20900 Oakwood Boulevard
P.O. Box 1970
Dearborn, Michigan 48124-4088
(313) 271-1620
*Restoration of Edison's Menlo Park laboratory, using many of the original artifacts.*

# CREDITS

Photographs in this book were provided courtesy of the U.S. Department of the Interior, National Park Service, Edison National Historic Site, unless otherwise noted below.

p. 10 (upper), Rutherford B. Hayes Presidential Center, Charles E. Frohman Collection; p. 17, Peter Newark's American Pictures; p. 19, From the Collections of Henry Ford Museum & Greenfield Village; p. 35 (upper), courtesy Thomas A. Edison Papers, Rutgers University; p. 35 (lower), The Granger Collection, New York; p. 36, Schenectady Museum; p.37 (inset), Schenectady Museum; p. 38, Consolidated Edison Company of New York; p. 41 (inset), Breton Littlehales, courtesy George Eastman House; p. 60-61, Breton Littlehales, courtesy Edison National Historic Site, p. 62 upper courtesy Yesterday's Treasures, New Market, Maryland.

## ACKNOWLEDGMENTS

The author and the publisher gratefully acknowledge the generous help and support of the whole staff of the Edison National Historic Site for their review of the text and layout and for their assistance in supplying pictures. The publisher also thanks Erika Glover, Granger Collection; Gilbert Gonzalez, Rutherford B. Hayes Presidential Center; Chris Hunter, Schenectady Museum; Peter Newark, Peter Newark's American Pictures; and Bob Rosenberg, Thomas A. Edison Papers, Rutgers University.

# INDEX

## EDUCATIONAL EXTENSIONS

1. If you were Thomas Edison, what would be your proudest accomplishment? Why?

2. In what ways does the book's text enable you to experience the life and times of Thomas Edison? Give examples, and note whether they are primary or secondary sources.

3. Summarize Thomas Edison's life and contributions to society. How do his contributions affect your daily life?

4. Discuss the meanings behind these two Thomas Edison quotes:

   "My mother taught me how to read good books quickly and correctly. And this opened up a great world of literature. I have always been very thankful for this early training."

   "Genius is 1 percent inspiration and 99 percent perspiration."

### MORE TO PONDER...

- What scientific and historic concepts or ideas are presented in the book? How does the author use evidence to support claims?

- What concepts or ideas would you like to learn more about?

- Who are the inventors that shaped and continue to shape our society?

- How do inventions affect our daily lives?

- What do inventors from the past and present have in common?